MORRILL ELEMENTARY SCHOOL

34880000804851

DATE DUE

92
MOS

Carrigan, Mellonee.

Carol Moseley-Braun

CAROL MOSELEY-BRAUN
Breaking Barriers

CAROL MOSELEY-BRAUN
Breaking Barriers

By Mellonee Carrigan

CHILDRENS PRESS ®
CHICAGO

To my parents, Gracie and Robert McKenzie.

*Special thanks to my sister,
Roslyn Morgan Russell, and to my friends
and others who supported my efforts.*

PHOTO CREDITS

Cover: Courtesy Senator Carol Moseley-Braun
AP/Wide World—2, 5, 16, 24 (both photos), 31
The Bettmann Archive—11
Moseley-Braun Family Collection—7 (top), 18
© Cameramann International, Ltd.—7 (bottom), 12
Reprinted with permission from the *Chicago Sun-Times*, © 1993—30
Courtesy Illinois Secretary of State Office—20
Reuters/Bettmann—1, 3, 27, 28, 32
© Terry Farmer/Tony Stone Images—21
Courtesy University of Illinois at Chicago—17
UPI/Bettmann—14

EDITORIAL STAFF

Project Editor: Mark Friedman
Design and Electronic Composition: Biner Design
Photo Editor: Jan Izzo

Library of Congress Cataloging-in-Publication Data
Carrigan, Mellonee
    Carol Moseley-Braun: breaking barriers/by Mellonee Carrigan.
    p. cm. — (Picture story biography)
    ISBN 0-516-04190-8
    1. Moseley-Braun, Carol, 1947—Juvenile literature. 2. Legislators—United States—Biography—Juvenile literature. 3. United States. Congress. Senate—Biography—Juvenile literature. 4. Afro-American legislators—Biography— Juvenile literature. [1. Moseley-Braun, Carol, 1947- . 2. Legislators. 3. Afro-Americans—Biography. 4.Women—Biography.] I. Title. II. Title: Carol Moseley-Braun. III. Series: Picture-story biographies.

E840.8.M67C37   1994   93-43869
328.73'092—dc20   CIP
[B]   AC

"CAROL! CAROL! CAROL!"

The familiar chant echoed over and over. The deafening applause grew louder. Carol Moseley-Braun waved triumphantly and flashed a brilliant smile. Hundreds of eager supporters at her Chicago campaign headquarters stomped and clapped wildly.

They shouted her name:

"Carol! Carol! Carol!"

At last, still smiling broadly, Carol stepped forward to give her victory speech. The people present were witnessing history: Carol Moseley-Braun was the first African American woman to be elected to the United States Senate.

"We have won a great victory tonight," the senator-elect told her cheering supporters on election night.

"You have made history. You are showing the way for our entire country to the future. You have shown what we can do when we come together. When we stop them from dividing us along race lines and gender lines.

"We put together a campaign, one that they said couldn't be done. Well, we did it! I'm going to work hard to be the best senator Illinois has ever had."

Carol was born on Aug. 14, 1947, to Joseph and Edna Moseley. She was the oldest of four children. Her family lived on the South Side of Chicago in a

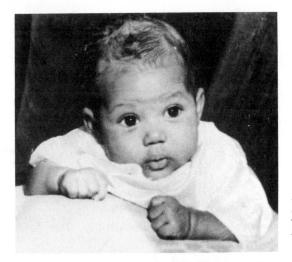

Left, Carol Moseley at a very young age. Below, the Moseleys' neighborhood on Chicago's South Side

neighborhood of mostly black working-class and middle-class families.

The Moseleys owned an apartment building. Carol's family lived on the first floor. Her "extended family" occupied the other apartments. Everyone who lived in the building was considered family, even though they were not all relatives of the Moseleys.

Joseph Moseley was a police officer. His brothers were police officers too. In the 1940s and 1950s, there were very few blacks on the Chicago police force. Joseph and his brothers were among the first blacks to integrate the force.

In the 1960s, Joseph quit the police force to work as a real estate salesman on the South Side. He was also active in politics and unions. He worked hard to integrate Chicago's schools, streetcar workers, and jail guards.

Sometimes Carol would attend meetings with her father. She learned her first lessons in politics while she was still a young girl. Joseph believed government could do a better job of serving the people, and that people should work actively for change in government and society.

Joseph Moseley often found himself frustrated by his hard work and political efforts. Sometimes he was so angry that he took his frustration out on his children, especially Carol. He would grow violent and beat the children with a rope or his fist. Sometimes he even waved guns at his family.

Carol would often take her three younger siblings and flee to her grandmother's house. Carol learned to be a peacemaker among her family—a skill she would later use as a politician.

Carol's mother worked full-time as a medical technician. It was a job held by very few women or blacks at the time.

Edna Moseley believed strongly in her duty to her family, but she was often unable to cope with her husband's mood swings and abusive behavior. Young Carol was frequently left in charge of the other children.

When Carol was eight years old, her family moved to a different neighborhood on the South Side. Carol became friends with a young white girl who lived next door. Their bedroom windows were opposite each other, and the girls would talk to each other through the window.

One day Carol found her friend crying. Her parents had spanked her for playing with a black girl. This was Carol's first experience with racial prejudice, and she felt terrible.

Carol continued encountering racism through her childhood. Her family took a trip to the South, where many states were still segregated. Blacks were not allowed to use the same bathrooms or drinking fountains as whites, and black children had to go to separate schools than white children. In Montgomery, Alabama, Carol

Segregation laws in the South forced blacks to use different water fountains than whites.

refused to drink from a "colored" drinking fountain because she felt the segregation laws were wrong.

Carol also experienced racial discrimination as a young student in Chicago public schools. Her elementary school had recently been integrated, and some white people were angered by the presence of black

Ruggles School in Chicago, where Carol attended grade school

children. Carol remembers that when
angry whites threw rocks at the school
windows, she and her classmates had
to duck under their desks to hide from
the rocks and shattered glass.

When she was fifteen years old,
Carol's parents divorced. Her father
sold their house and moved away. This
made Carol very sad. Although he was
sometimes abusive and violent, Carol

admired and loved her father dearly. The family was then forced to move out of their middle-class neighborhood.

Carol's family went to live with her grandmother in the Oakwood neighborhood on the South Side. It was a slum nicknamed "Bucket of Blood." It was the first time Carol had lived among very poor blacks in a violent neighborhood.

Carol made some friends in her new environment, but she spent most of her time alone. She tried to get away from Oakwood as often as she could. She would sometimes take her mother's car without her knowing it and go for a drive.

Carol worked as a checker in a grocery store during high school to help her mother pay bills. Meanwhile, her mother worked hard and saved all the money she could. She wanted to move the family as far away from the Oakwood ghetto as possible.

In 1966, Dr. Martin Luther King, Jr., led a civil rights march near Carol's neighborhood. Carol, a teenager, joined Dr. King's protest against racial discrimination. Angry crowds that opposed Dr. King showed up and attacked the marchers by throwing rocks.

Carol fell to her knees and shielded her head from the rocks. Dr. King was only a few feet away from where she knelt. Carol watched as King was hit by a

Martin Luther King, Jr., is hit by a rock, but he marches on.

rock . . . but he ignored the blow and kept on marching.

Carol was furious at the whites. She wanted to pick up a rock and throw it back. Then she remembered that Dr. King stood for nonviolence. The quiet dignity that King showed that day left a deep impression on young Carol.

Carol was a teenager in the turbulent 1960s. Angry blacks were staging protests, marches, and sit-ins against racial segregation.

Carol fought her own small battles against segregation. She once staged a sit-in at an all-white restaurant. Although the restaurant had a rule against serving blacks, Carol walked in, took a seat, and refused to leave until she was served a cup of coffee. When the coffee finally arrived, Carol did not drink it. She considered it a victory that she had been served. She put a quarter on the counter and left.

Chicago civil rights marchers are pelted with rocks.

Carol also tried to integrate Rainbow Beach, an all-white beach on Chicago's lakefront. A mob again pelted her group of protesters with rocks. This time, with courage inspired by Martin Luther King, Carol ignored the rocks and the vicious shouts and continued her protest.

Carol's civil rights activities worried her mother and made her nervous. But Carol's father gave her encouragement. He was her biggest supporter.

Carol's friends began to join militant black groups such as the Black Panthers. The Panthers believed in using violence to end segregation. But Carol agreed to help only with the Panthers' breakfast programs. She was committed to live by Dr. King's message of nonviolence.

After graduating from high school, Carol attended the University of Illinois at Chicago. She participated in a number of activities, and she was elected to the student government on a multiracial ticket.

The University of Illinois at Chicago

After college, Carol enrolled at the University of Chicago Law School. While in law school, she organized the Black Law Students Association. She was the organization's first president.

In law school, she also began dating a young law student named Michael Braun. In 1973, one year after Carol completed law school, she and Michael

Carol shows off son Matthew.

were married. They later had a son and named him Matthew.

Carol worked as an assistant attorney for three years in the U.S. Attorney's office. Her success as a young prosecutor earned her the U.S. Attorney General's Special Achievement Award. She also worked as an assistant for the Davis, Niner & Barnhill law firm.

Carol had risen out of the South Side ghetto, completed her education, and become a successful lawyer. But her life would soon change even more dramatically. In 1977, some of her neighbors asked her to run for political office. She had little experience in politics, but she agreed to run.

In 1978, Carol was elected to the Illinois State House of Representatives. She suddenly found herself in Springfield, the Illinois state capital, where she spent the next ten years.

Carol immediately earned a reputation as a qualified legislator and a powerful debater. She was an advocate for more efficient government and improving education. Her hallmark was her ability to build coalitions—to bring together people of different political beliefs or races and make them work for a common cause.

In 1983, Carol became legislative floor leader in Springfield for Harold Washington, Chicago's first black mayor.

A 1985 photo of Carol, when she was an Illinois state representative

The State House of Representatives in Springfield, Illinois

In her new position, Carol was the chief sponsor of bills to reform education and to ban racial discrimination in housing and private clubs.

During her ten years in the Illinois General Assembly, Carol received many awards, including being voted "Best Legislator" in every year of her term.

After just two terms in the House, Carol became the first African American and the first woman to serve as assistant House majority leader.

Carol had become a skillful and experienced politician. But in 1986, Carol's private life began to crumble. She and Michael were divorced, although they remained friends. Her mother had a leg amputated and was confined to a wheelchair. Carol's beloved brother, Johnny, died of alcohol and drug abuse. And following these tragedies, her father also died. It was the worst time of Carol's life.

Carol responded to her personal sadness by throwing herself into her work. Her political ambition grew even stronger. She did not plan to stay in the state legislature forever. She wanted to move on to bigger challenges.

Her chance came in 1987, when Mayor Washington had Carol

nominated for the office of Cook County Recorder of Deeds. This important office oversees all the real estate records for Chicago and Cook County. In 1988, Carol won her election for Recorder of Deeds with more than one million votes cast in her favor. She was the first woman and the first African American to hold executive office in Cook County government.

Carol took over an inefficient office and whipped it into shape. She had all the records computerized, and she adopted a code of ethics for the office.

As Carol broke racial and gender ground in her political career, the mood of the country was also changing. In 1991, Clarence Thomas, a black Republican, was nominated for a seat on the U.S. Supreme Court. Many people opposed Thomas's confirmation because he had been accused of sexual harassment by Anita Hill, his former

Anita Hill (left) testifies before the Senate Judiciary Committee at the confirmation hearings for Supreme Court nominee Clarence Thomas (right).

employee. The entire nation watched on television as dramatic Senate hearings highlighted the issues of racism, women's rights, and sexual harassment.

Thomas was eventually confirmed. Illinois Senator Alan Dixon voted for Thomas, a decision that angered women's groups. They felt he had ignored the women's perspective in the debate by believing Clarence Thomas's testimony over Anita Hill's. They vowed to block his re-election in 1992.

Carol Moseley-Braun began getting calls and letters from many people, blacks and whites. They urged her to run in the state primary election. Carol had also opposed the nomination of Clarence Thomas. As she watched the Thomas confirmation hearings on television, she was angered by the feeling that the U.S. Senate was an elite "club" comprised almost entirely of upper-class white men.

Carol felt that Americans were ready for a change. She believed government should be more responsible and open to all people.

Carol wanted to take a new voice to the Senate—the voice of working people. And she felt she was the best person for the job.

With no money or political backing, Carol launched a grass-roots campaign on November 19, 1991, to run for the U.S. Senate.

Enthusiastic voters began lining up at campaign stops to shake Carol's hand and offer their encouragement. Wherever Carol went, she delivered rousing campaign speeches, and she was greeted by supportive crowds.

A December 1991 poll showed Dixon running ahead of Carol by a two-to-one margin. Powerful political groups, the media, and the vast majority of voters had hardly even noticed her candidacy.

Carol got a lucky break when Al Hofeld, a wealthy Chicago lawyer, joined the race. He mounted an expensive ad campaign against Dixon. Dixon and Hofeld bitterly attacked each other, but Carol watched these quarrels from the sidelines. Carol carried out a positive campaign

Carol on the campaign trail

emphasizing issues of public concern. She refused to engage in "negative campaigning."

After months of trailing Dixon in every poll, Carol scored a shocking come-from-behind victory. On March 17, 1992, she won the Illinois Democratic Primary election. She had

*At a Chicago rally, thousands cheer Carol, Bill Clinton, and Al Gore.
Clinton and Gore went on to win the presidential election in 1992.*

done what many people believed was
impossible.

As she took the stage for her victory
speech, she danced to the tune of "Ain't
No Stopping Us Now." She became a
nationwide, overnight sensation.

But the real test was still to come: the
general election.

Carol's opponent was Republican Richard Williamson. He launched a negative campaign against Carol, calling her a typical, big-spending liberal who couldn't be trusted. Late in the campaign, it was revealed that Carol's mother had received $29,000 from investments, but Carol had failed to report the income to the government or pay taxes on it. Williamson pounced on this issue and attempted to turn it into a major scandal.

Carol fought hard and defended herself against Williamson. Her faith and determination were stronger than ever. She felt that it was her duty to use her talents to help people. Her simple message of hope and her down-to-earth style appealed to all kinds of voters—blacks and whites, women and men. Even Republican voters crossed party lines and decided to cast their votes for the Democratic candidate.

On November 3, 1992, Carol made history once more. She was elected to the United States Senate. She defeated Rich Williamson with 53 percent of the vote.

She took office on January 5, 1993, becoming the first black woman and only the fourth black in U.S. history to

Carol celebrates on election night with her mother (right) and son Matthew (left).

Carol and Senator Diane Feinstein (right) were the first women to serve on the Senate Judiciary Committee.

serve in the Senate. She quickly established herself as a fine senator and a staunch supporter of civil rights.

Carol Mosely-Braun's remarkable career proves that one person can overcome discrimination against race and gender. In one of the country's most powerful legislative bodies, she is still breaking barriers.

CAROL MOSELEY-BRAUN

1947	August 14—born in Chicago, Illinois
1964	Graduated from high school
1966	Marched with Dr. Martin Luther King, Jr.
1969	Graduated from the University of Illinois at Chicago
1970	Speech writer for Illinois State Senator Richard Newhouse
1972	Graduated from the University of Chicago Law School
1973	Married law school classmate Michael Braun
1976	Son Matthew born
1978	Elected to the Illinois State House of Representatives and served ten years
1983	Named legislative floor leader for Chicago Mayor Harold Washington
1986	Divorced from Michael Braun
1988	Elected Cook County Recorder of Deeds
1992	Elected to the United States Senate

INDEX

ABOUT THE AUTHOR

Mellonee Carrigan attended the University of Arkansas at Fayetteville, Arkansas. She received a Bachelor of Arts degree in journalism. Ms. Carrigan's background includes work as a copy editor for *Electronic Media* newspaper in Chicago. She was a news reporter and national broadcast news writer/editor for United Press International in Chicago. She was also a reporter for the City News Bureau of Chicago.

In addition, Ms. Carrigan has written free-lance articles for the *Chicago Tribune* and *Metro New York* magazine. She also received a certificate in television studio production.

Ms. Carrigan's hobbies include reading, bike riding, and competitive running. She has completed two Chicago marathons and numerous other races. She presently resides in Chicago.